ADVENTURES IN WRITING:

A FUN GUIDE TO FIGURATIVE LANGUAGE

**Children's
Creative Writing
Institute**

AUTHOR: JENNIFER WOOLF

DESIGN: JÉRÔME CURCHOD

ISBN# 978-0-692-24486-9   © 2017 The Children's Creative Writing Institute

TABLE OF CONTENTS

INTRODUCTION

This book contains all of the writing tricks you knew were there. One by one, you'll unlock the secrets of the universe and learn how to create your own hyperbolic statements, amazing alliterations and more. This book is like the map to a hidden treasure.

If you've ever stayed up late at night wondering what in the world an onomatopoeia is, you can rest easy now. The answer is just pages away.

Every chapter has an explanation, example, worksheets and a fun activity. Who knew writing could be so much fun?

Yes, there is a technical term. All of these literary devices fall under the umbrella of **FIGURATIVE LANGUAGE**. However, if you say the phrase "figurative language" to random people on the street, nine out of ten of them will look at you like you have two heads. Actually, I just made that statistic up, but if you decide to do this, please let us know how it goes.

Wait, did you just say that figurative language is an umbrella? Nope. It's a metaphor. Read on and you'll know what that means.

Before we start, let's play a little matching game and see how much you already know. Draw a line connecting the sentence to the type of figurative writing that it represents.

1) **Idiom** —————————— a) This book is so much fun it will knock your socks off.

2) **Alliteration** b) This book is fantastic, funny and fabulous.

3) **Hyperbole** c) This book is like a treasure chest.

4) **Simile** d) Wow! I love this book.

5) **Metaphor** e) This is the best book in the whole wide world.

6) **Onomatopoeia** f) Thud! The book landed on my desk with a thud.

7) **Interjection** g) This book talks to me and makes figurative writing come alive.

8) **Personification** h) This book will shine a light on fun ways to write.

1 = a; 2 = b; 3 = e; 4 = c; 5 = h; 6 = f; 7 = d; 8 = g

METAPHOR

PERSONIFICATION

HYPERBOLE

INTERJECTION

IDIOM

SIMILE

ALLITERATION

ONOMATOPOEIA

HYPERBOLE

GO BIG

Hyperbole is just a fancy way of saying really big, huge exaggeration.

Examples:

I've told you to make your bed a million times.

I have so much homework that it's going to take me a decade to finish it.

FILL IN THE BLANKS HYPERBOLE

Use the words in the box to fill in the blanks

1. My books weigh a _____ .

2. I'm so hungry I could eat a _____ .

3. He's taller than a _____ .

4. That joke is so _____ the last time I heard it I almost fell off my _____ .

5. He's so fast that he can run faster than a _____ .

6. My school is _____ miles from my house and I have to walk _____ both ways.

giraffe   dinosaur   ton

race car   up hill

old   five-hundred   horse

UNDERSTATED/OVERSTATED

The opposite of hyperbole is understatement. Have you ever known someone who downplays everything?

Rewrite the following sentences twice. Yes, twice. The first time, make it understated, okay boring, and the second time use the greatest hyperbole in the history of hyperbole.

1. **Describe a hot day.**

   It's a little warm out.

   It's so hot my shoes are going to melt.

2. **It snowed yesterday.**

3. **The players on the other basketball team were tall.**

4. **I'm thirsty.**

5. **It's a long drive to my grandmother's house.**

EVERYONE'S A COMEDIAN

Hyperbole is a classic tool that comedians use. Here are two examples. Let's see if you can come up with two of your own.

- My pimple is so big it should have its own zip code.

- I have to get up so early that my alarm clock wakes me up half an hour before I even go to sleep.

YOUR TURN
The trick here is to make the exaggeration really big and really silly.

1)

2)

Write a paragraph describing one of the following. Use as many details as you can, and by all means, get completely and totally carried away with your hyperboles.

A REALLY BORING SCHOOL ASSEMBLY • THE BEST RESTAURANT MEAL YOU EVER HAD • HOW NICE YOUR BEST FRIEND IS • HOW BAD THE GYM AT YOUR SCHOOL SMELLS

Create your own hyperbole.
It can be about anything you want.

Illustrate your hyperbole.

ACTIVITY TIME

HYPERBOLE HUNT

Whether you are watching TV, playing with your friends or at the dinner table, find three examples of hyperbole. Hint: commercials are a really good place to look.

1.

2.

3.

PULL A FAST ONE

Go up to someone and say, "My, you're looking very hyperbolic today." If they smile and say "Thank you," then you'll know that they have no idea what hyperbole is.

HYPERBOLE AND ME

Turn yourself into a superhero! Using hyperbole, write a paragraph describing yourself. Remember, the object here is to GO BIG. Go ahead and give yourself the ability to jump to the stratosphere or hear a whispered conversation in another state.

HYPERBOLE

IS THE SUPERHERO OF FIGURATIVE LANGUAGE.

WRITING PROMPTS

1. You have just invented the "Hyperbolator." It's a machine that lets you type in an ordinary phrase and it spits out a hyperbolic version. Are you going to keep it to yourself or are you going to share it with the world? Describe your machine and how you plan to use it.

2. Write a first person story from the point of view of a goldfish whose bowl sits on the kitchen counter. Use at least 3 hyperboles.

3. Use hyperbole to describe the most disgusting meal you've ever had.

4. You just found out that you are moving to Mars. Use hyperbole to describe what moving day will be like.

Use the following pages for these prompts or create your own.

ONOMATOPOEIA

Onomatopoeia is a word that sounds like what it's describing. Think of it as sound effects for words.

Onomatopoeia is the best word in the English language. Try to say it three times fast without giggling. You can't! Better yet, close your eyes and try to spell it.

Examples:

"Quack," said the duck.

My shoes squeaked on the gym floor.

Match these onomatopoeias with the correct picture.

ROAR

TICK TOCK

TWEET

POP

SPLASH

CHOO-CHOO

Onomatopoeias can be used with exclamation points, as dialogue or as plain, old description. Fill in the blanks with your own onomatopoeias.

1. _____ The sound startled me and I turned around to see my little brother standing next to a pile of fallen cereal boxes.

2. At the zoo, I heard one pig say, "_____"and the other respond with a louder, "_____".

3. He was such a noisy eater that everyone in the restaurant could hear him _____ his soup.

Write and illustrate your own onomatopoeias.

1. _____

_____

2. _____

_____

3. _____

_____

Here's the boring sentence.
Rewrite it using onomatopoeia.
Use as many extra details as you can.

1. **The train was loud.**

   Choo choo! The train was so loud, I jumped when

   I heard "choo choo".

2. **My brother sneezed in the middle of the concert.**

3. **The lady sitting next to me at the concert gave me a funny look when I ate my potato chips.**

4. **My dad has a very loud laugh.**

5. **There are so many keys on this keychain that they make noise.**

6. **The car stopped suddenly and made a loud sound.**

ONOMATOPOEIA PARAGRAPH

Write a descriptive paragraph using at least 5 onomatopoeias.

Here are some ideas: *A day at the beach, A trip to the zoo, A train ride, A massive traffic jam, A thunder and lightning storm.*

ACTIVITY TIME
ONOMATOPOEIA COMPETITION

This game can be played with anywhere from 2 people to one million. Okay, that might be a little bit of hyperbole, but you get the idea. Divide your players into teams. If you only have two people, obviously you will only have two teams.

We all know how heated onomatopoeia competitions can get, so shake hands before you start and agree to be friends after the match.

Set a timer for 5 minutes and write as many onomatopoeias as you can think of. Give yourself 1 point for each three letter onomatopoeia, 3 points for each four letter onomatopoeia, and 6 points for any onomatopoeia with more than 5 letters.

Buzz 3   Moo 1   Crash 6   Splat 6

SCORE   16

TEAM:

_____   _____   _____   _____

_____   _____   _____   _____

_____   _____   _____   _____

_____   _____   _____   _____

_____   _____   _____   _____

_____   _____   _____   _____

SCORE [   ]

TEAM:

_____   _____   _____   _____

_____   _____   _____   _____

_____   _____   _____   _____

_____   _____   _____   _____

_____   _____   _____   _____

_____   _____   _____   _____

SCORE [   ]

tinkle

honk

drip

moan

splash

poof

pitter-patter

splat

crash

buzz

roar

hiss

ding-dong

zip

smash

peep

ONOMATOPOEIA

click

slurp

growl

boing

meow

snap

murmur

squish

whiz

hush

clang

pop

sizzle

chirp

thud

clap

woosh

bang

ha-ha

achoo

WRITING PROMPTS

1. Describe a day in the life of a very clumsy person. Use at least 3 onomatopoeias.

2. Describe a storm that starts off with a drizzle and gets harder and harder, finally ending with thunder and lightening.

3. What is the quietest onomatopoeia you can think of? Start a story with it.

4. A waiter carrying a large tray of full plates and glasses slips on a banana peel. Describe the scene using at least 5 onomatopoeias.

Use the following pages for these prompts or create your own.

PERSONIFICATION

Personification is giving human characteristics to objects, ideas or even concepts.

Examples:

The grass danced in the gentle spring breeze.

Time marches on.

The thought jumped into my brain.

Personification makes your words dance, and helps create an emotional connection with your readers.

Fill in the blanks using words from the box.

1. The blades of grass were _____ in the wind.

2. The carrot _____ at me and _____ me not to take a bite.

3. The school bell _____ and I jumped ten feet.

4. The thunder _____ as the raindrops started to fall.

5. The clouds _____ together in a group.

6. The bird _____ a song to me.

sang   screamed

dared   huddled

roared   glared   dancing

PUT YOUR PENCILS TO WORK

Personification will put an extra bounce in your writing. Rewrite the following sentences using personification.

1. **The toaster is broken.**

The toaster refused to make my toast this morning.

2. **The moon was bright.**

_____

3. **The keyboard made noise as I typed.**

_____

4. **The drums were loud.**

_____

5. **The trees were blowing around in the wind.**

_____

This page is staring at you, waiting to see what you will write and draw. Look around the room and pick an object to personify. Or, you can close your eyes and pull something out of your imagination.

Write four examples of personification and illustrate them.

1.
_____

_____

2.
_____

_____

3.
_____

_____

4.
_____

_____

Write a descriptive essay about an object you use or wear every day. Include at least two examples of personification. You can use one of the suggestions below or come up with your own.

backpack   toothbrush

pencil   alarm clock   sidewalk

book   cereal   computer

ACTIVITY TIME

MIX AND MATCH

Make two sets of index cards. I recommend using two different colors, but if you only have white index cards, just use two different color crayons. One color will be for nouns and the other will be for verbs. You'll want to have at least 10 cards for each, but the more you have, the better. If you only have two players, each player will write 5 nouns and 5 verbs. If you have more players you can divide accordingly. Use the list for some suggestions.

Shuffle the cards and let the first player take one of each. Now everyone has to make a personification sentence using those words. They will definitely be silly because you have to work with randomly paired nouns and verbs. Let's see how creative you can be.

NOUNS	VERBS
cape	ran
cement	danced
brownie	called
toothpaste	frowned
car	smiled
turkey	jumped
fish	winked
waffle	yelled
moon	sang
phone	whistled

"I might be crazy, but I'm pretty sure the wet cement smiled as I carved my initials into it."

Keep your cards, and add to them each time you play this game.

The keyboard
yawned and
the screen
closed its eyes
in frustration
as I sat staring
off into space.

PERSONIFICATION

The keyboard
smiled and
the screen
jumped for
joy as I started
typing again.

WRITING PROMPTS

1. You are decorating for a birthday party, but the balloons keep getting away. Describe the situation and what you do about it.

2. You sit down to write in your journal, but can't seem to get started. Describe what the pencil and paper do or think.

3. It's a very windy day. Describe the wind, trees, grass and flowers.

4. Your baseball mitt is sitting on the table but you are focused on your homework. Describe the situation.

Use the following pages for these prompts or create your own.

SIMILES

A simile is a figure of speech that compares two things using the word "like" or "as".

That's the official definition. But the function of similes is much more exciting than that. Think of them as magic machines that can transform a boring description into something way more interesting. If writing is like painting a picture, similes are the paint. They help create vivid images for your readers.

Examples:

This chocolate milkshake tastes like heaven.

Her voice is as smooth as silk.

Complete each metaphor using words or phrases from the box.

a cat is screaming

rollercoaster

flowers

mud

silk

bird's nest

1. This old elevator is as bumpy as a _____ .

2. Her new hairstyle looks like a _____ .

3. My new blanket is so soft, it feels like _____ .

4. My mom's new perfume smells like _____ .

5. When my sister practices the violin, it sounds as if _____ .

6. Spinach tastes like _____ .

Using your senses is a great way to come up with similes.

1. The apple pie my grandmother just baked smells like _____ .

2. The apple pie my grandmother just baked looks like _____ .

3. The apple pie my grandmother just baked feels like _____ on my tongue.

4. The apple pie my grandmother just baked tastes like _____ .

5. The apple pie my grandmother just baked sounds like _____ .

(okay, that one's a little silly, unless it's a talking pie)

Here's the boring sentence.
Write a new one with a simile.

1. **He's slow.**

   He's as slow as a snail.

2. **The new car is fast.**

3. **The man is tall.**

4. **My friend has red hair.**

5. **It's hot out today.**

6. **The parade was fun.**

Write a paragraph describing an object. You can use the suggestion box or come up with your own.

the dumpster   my new bicycle
    the new principal at school
        school lunches
a bouquet of flowers

_____

_____

_____

_____

_____

_____

_____

ACTIVITY TIME

Writing is much more than sitting at a desk and putting words on a piece of paper. Sometimes the best thing you can do for your writing is to get outside and move around. You can dictate your answers into a recorder, you can jot them down on a piece of paper, or you can shout them into the wind.

Step 1: Go outside.

Step 2: Close your eyes and take ten deep breaths.

Step 3: Open your eyes and use a simile to describe something that you see.

Step 4: Close your eyes again and listen very carefully. Listen to all of the sounds around you and use similes to describe them.

Step 5: Feel something near you. It can be a tree trunk, a blade of grass, concrete or anything else. Use a simile to describe how it feels.

Step 6: Close your eyes again and inhale. Use a simile to describe what you smell. It can be flowers, trash, the kid standing next to you or many other things.

Step 7: Taste. Now it must be time for a snack! Describe what your snack tastes like.

SIMILE

is like the

HEART

&

SOUL

of figurative
language.

WRITING PROMPTS

1. There's a large spider on your pillow. Describe it using at least two similes.

2. You are making a sign for your lemonade stand and want everyone who passes by to know how delicious it is. Use "like" and "as" at least once each.

3. Your next door neighbor is a professional trumpet player and practices for many hours every day. Use at least two similes to describe what it sounds like.

4. You've just eaten the best chocolate chip cookie ever and you are trying to describe it to your friend. Use one simile for the gooey chocolate chips and one for the crunchy cookie.

Use the following pages for these prompts or create your own.

METAPHOR

A metaphor is a comparison that does not use the words *like* or *as*. Metaphors are very similar to similes, but they create stronger images and are usually more poetic. Instead of saying that the object is like something else, you are saying that it IS something else.

Examples:

That soccer player is a beast.
The snow blanketed the entire city.

Fill in the blanks with words from the box.

party   doll   nightmare

calculator   flowers   art

1. I am so glad we got a new principal. The last

one was a _____ .

2. My brother is a human _____ .

3. My peanut butter and marshmallow fluff sandwich

is a work of _____ .

4. Love is a bouquet of _____ .

5. My little sister is a _____ .

6. The marching band sounds like a _____ .

Use metaphors to describe 5 of your favorite people.

For example:

1. Jane is a ray of sunshine

2.

3.

4.

5.

6.

Here's the boring sentence.
Rewrite it with a metaphor.

1. **That house is big.**

   That house is a monster.

2. **My remote controlled helicopter is fun.**

3. **It's hot outside today.**

4. **My dog has a lot of energy.**

5. **Her shirt is colorful.**

6. **His sneeze was loud.**

METAPHOR BIOGRAPHY

Using metaphors, write a paragraph describing yourself. Here are some questions to get you started.

1. What kind of facial expression are you? A smile? A frown?

2. What type of shoes are you? Flip flops? Cleats? High heels?

3. What kind of musical instrument are you? Piano? Drums? Ukulele?

4. What kind of dessert are you? Pie? Ice cream? Cookies?

ACTIVITY TIME

Put away those pencils and stretch your legs. All you need for this game is an imagination, and you can play it anywhere, even in the car.

Most nouns can be described by many different metaphors. The first person comes up with the noun and the first metaphor and everyone else keep adding on to it, repeating all of the previous metaphors. How far can you go?

For example:

Tony Hawk is a flying machine.
Tony Hawk is a flying machine and a beast.
Tony Hawk is a flying machine, a beast and Superman.
Tony Hawk is a flying machine, a beast, Superman and a daredevil.
Tony Hawk is a flying machine, a beast, Superman, a daredevil and a legend.

METAPHOR is a CHAMPION

Metaphor

1. The sky is bright blue, with fluffy clouds. Use metaphors to paint the picture.

2. You are a spy and you've just been given a new gadget. Describe what it is and what it does using at least two metaphors.

3. Write a poem about a giant sea turtle using at least three metaphors.

4. Describe a peanut butter and jelly sandwich using metaphors for the bread, peanut butter, and jelly.

Use the following pages for these prompts or create your own.

ALLITERATION

Alliteration is when words in a phrase start with the same letter or sound. Alliterative phrases are fun to read and say. They roll right off of your tongue, unless, of course, they are tongue twisters.

Examples:

Pretty pink popsicle.

I love to sing silly songs.

Alliterations are amazing, awesome and astounding!

Use the words in the box to fill in the blanks and create alliterations.

little   delicious   bouncing
~~green~~
large   house
whispering   red

1. The <u>green</u> grass was wet.

2. Mary had a _____ lamb.

3. The _____ roses are beautiful.

4. That bakery sells _____ donuts.

5. That tree is full of _____ lemons.

6. The haunted _____ has _____ walls.

7. The _____ ball got away from me.

ALLITERATION AVENUE
HOW FAR CAN YOU GO?

Ask Alice about alliteration.

Barbie baked banana bread.

C

D

E

F

G

H

I

J

K

ALLITERATION AVENUE

L _____

M _____

N _____

O _____

P _____

Q _____

R _____

S _____

T _____

U _____

V _____

W _____

X _____

Y _____

Z _____

ALLITERATION MENU

Daisy Davis is opening her first restaurant.

She wants all of her items to be alliterative. Write a paragraph describing the restaurant and some of the menu items. You can use alliteration to describe the food, and also the décor. Be as silly as you like, but try to make the restaurant sound like a place you would like to have dessert. In other words, please don't put any zany zebras or wacky walruses on the menu.

DAISY'S DESSERT DIVE

*You can find us on the corner of Alliteration Alley
and Boulangerie Boulevard.
Daisy's Dessert Dive is the best place for delicious snacks.
Come visit us after school, after dinner or any time at all.
We serve all of your favorite desserts and drinks.*

ACTIVITY TIME

Super Secret Alliteration Assignment

Start sneaking alliterations into your conversations and see if anyone notices. It'll be like your own secret joke.

Johnny: "Please pass the purple pencil."
Susan: "What's so funny?"
Johnny: "Um...nothing."

On the other hand, if Susan says,
"Sure, and here's a cranberry colored crayon," it's game on.

How many alliterations have you used today?

What's the longest alliteration you've ever made?

ZANY ZEBRA

LEAPING LION

ANGRY ALLIGATOR

HUNGRY HIPPO

CHEERFUL CHEETAH

KIND KOALA

WRITING PROMPTS

1. A crayon company has asked you to name its new crayon. Describe the color and give it an alliterative name that has at least three words.

2. Describe your family, giving everyone an alliterative nickname.

3. We all know that Peter Piper picked a peck of pickled peppers, but the world needs more tongue twisters. Write your own tongue twister.

4. Use as much alliteration as you can to tell about your recent trip to Mars.

Use the following pages for these prompts or create your own.

INTERJECTIONS

An interjection is a small word that packs a big punch. It's used to express a strong emotion such as surprise, joy, anger or pain. They are usually followed by exclamation points, but sometimes a comma will do.

Examples:

Yum! That was a delicious pie.

Cool! His skateboard glows in the dark.

Aw, the baby panda is adorable.

Add the correct interjection using words from the box.

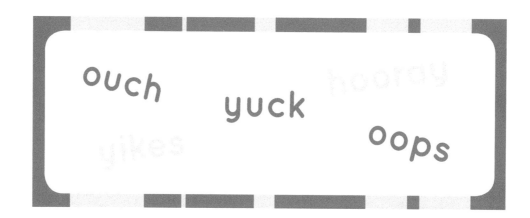

1. _____ I dropped the jar of spaghetti sauce.

2. _____ I just found out that I won the writing contest.

3. _____ That is the most disgusting looking meatloaf I have ever seen.

4. _____ I burned myself on the hot plate.

5. _____ I'm really scared to see if there is a monster under my bed.

Interjections definitely add pop to your writing, but you have to remember that too much of a good thing is usually just too much.

Think of them like chili peppers. They add a lot of flavor but you don't want to overdo it, otherwise you'll end up sounding like this:

Wow! Sheesh! Golly! The little boy was so excited about his new bicycle that he couldn't stop blurting out interjections.

Add an interjection before the following sentence and illustrate.

1. _____ My sister screamed when she realized that I borrowed her shirt without asking.

2. _____ I won the lottery.

3. _____ The teacher kept telling us to be quiet during the assembly.

4. _____ I heard a hissing sound as my friend was trying to get my attention.

Here's the interjection. You write the sentence.

Awesome!

_____

Whew!

_____

Oh no! _____

Wait! _____

Sorry! _____

Yikes! _____

Hey! _____

INTERJECTION CONVERSATION

Writing dialogue is a lot of fun because you can really let your characters' personalities show.

Write dialogue between two very enthusiastic friends. Everything they say starts with an interjection. Have them talk about tomorrow's school field trip to the beach.

For example:

Beatrice: "Ughhhh! I can't believe she's making us do homework before our field trip."

Henrietta: "Unbelievable! That takes a lot of nerve."

_____

_____

_____

_____

_____

_____

_____

ACTIVITY TIME

Finally, a game that doesn't require any equipment. No paper. No pencils. No timers or anything else. You can play this game in the car, waiting in line or just about anywhere.

All you have to do is start everything you say with an interjection. When you forget to use an interjection, you're out. The last player remaining in the game wins. Ha! This isn't going to be as easy as you think.

Oh no

Yikes

Ugh

Ouch

Shoot

Darn

Eek

Wow

Hooray

INTERJECTIONS

Whoa

Rats

Wait

Whew

Oops

Bravo

Yipee

Yuck

WRITING PROMPTS

1.   Write a story that starts with the interjection, "Hooray!"

2.   Imagine that you are allowed to order a triple scoop ice cream cone. Write a paragraph describing it that uses at least two interjections.

3.   Write a story from the point of view of a ghost. Do not use the interjections "Yikes" or "Boo." Use at least three other interjections.

4.   Start a story with the interjection, "Shhhh!" Also use "Oops" and "Ow."

Use the following pages for these prompts or create your own.

IDIOMS

An idiom is an expression whose meaning is different than the literal meanings of the words. Idioms give flavor and personality to your writing. Actually, they're a lot of fun in everyday conversations, too.

Idioms become part of a dialect, or the way locals express themselves. The idioms in England are very different from the idioms in California. If you tell someone in California that you are going to hang ten, they know you are going surfing. If someone from England tells you that your outfit is brilliant, they don't mean that your shirt is smart.

Examples:

In a pickle

This is an expression that means that you have a problem or a tricky situation.

I'm all ears

This means that you are ready to listen very carefully.

MATCHING IDIOMS

match these idioms with their literal meanings

nest egg   someone who lies around

the last straw   a lot of money

an arm and a leg   that's it, no more chances

lending an ear   savings

couch potato   listening

Imagine how confusing it would be if we took idioms literally.
We'd be stealing from bird's nests, buying lots of extra straws,
putting potatoes on our sofas, cutting off our arms and legs
to pay for things and then cutting off our ears when someone
asks us to listen to them.

ANIMAL IDIOMS

There are lots and lots of idioms that involve animals. Use context clues to guess what these idioms mean and write your definition on the lines.

1. I was late to dinner and by the time I got there, there were only a few crumbs left. My mom shrugged and said, "Well, **the early bird catches the worm.**"

_____

2. We stopped in an antique store but my little sister had so much energy she was like a **bull in a china shop**. We had to leave quickly.

_____

3. The boy next to me kept looking at my test and cheating. I'll never sit next to that **copycat** again.

_____

4. This might be an interesting game. The Lakers are definitely the **underdogs**, but I think they can get it done.

_____

5. When my teacher walked into the classroom and saw us all sitting quietly at our desks she got suspicious and said, **"Something's fishy."**

_____

Here's the boring way to say it.
Rewrite each sentence with an idiom.

1. **I'm hoarse.** There's a frog in my throat

2. **I'm really nervous.**

3. **I don't feel well.**

4. **I'm tired.**

5. **That was easy.**

6. **I'm sorry that I cursed.**

Answer key:
There is more than one correct answer.
Here are some suggestions.

2. I have butterflies in my stomach. 3. I'm under the weather. 4. I'm pooped. 5. That was a piece of cake. 6. Excuse my French.

A BIG MISUNDERSTANDING

Write a story about a misunderstanding that occurred when someone didn't know the meaning of an idiom. For example, in one of the Amelia Bedelia stories, the owner of the house tells Amelia to prune the hedges. This means to trim the bushes, but Amelia takes it literally and sticks prunes on the hedges.

You can use one of these idioms or one of your own.

Piece of cake
(something that is easy)

Put a sock in it
(stop talking)

Spilling the beans
(telling a secret)

Back seat driver
(someone who tells the driver what to do)

ACTIVITY TIME
IDIOM CHARADES

This game is a piece of cake to put together and time will fly because you will have so much fun.

You will need:
- A timer
- A piece of paper to keep score
- A pencil
- Index cards with idioms written on them.

Divide your group into two teams. You can flip a coin or do rock-paper-scissors to decide who goes first. The team that goes first picks a card and has two minutes to make sure everyone understands the idiom and make a strategy to act it out. The other team has four minutes to figure it out. Sometimes it will be as obvious as an elephant in the room and sometimes you will have to take a stab in the dark.

If the team guesses the correct idiom before the 4 minutes are up, they get a point.

ALTERNATIVE
If you just want to have some fun and not fight tooth and nail or be at each other's throats, there's no need to keep score. Simply yell the correct idiom and reward yourselves with a round of applause.

WARNING
You might have so much fun that you will end up cracking each other up.

WRITING PROMPTS

1. Write a story that starts with some saying, "A penny for your thoughts."

2. Describe an object, gadget or idea that is the "best thing since sliced bread."

3. Describe something you thought was going to be difficult but turned out to be "a piece of cake."

4. To be "bull headed" means to be stubborn. "Hold your horses" means you need to be patient and wait. Write a story that uses both of these idioms.

Use the following pages for these prompts or create your own.

MIXING IT UP

It's going to radically rock your world when I tell you that one sentence can have two types of figurative language. You've made it this far, so you've probably noticed that the previous sentence contains an idiom and an alliteration. Whoa! How cool is that? Now it's your turn.

1. Create a sentence with an alliteration and hyperbole.

_____

_____

2. Create a sentence with an onomatopoeia and a simile.

_____

_____

3. Create a sentence with an idiom and a metaphor.

_____

_____

4. Create a sentence with personification and onomatopoeia.

_____

_____

5. Create a sentence with an interjection and a simile.

_____

_____

FREE FOR ALL

Now is the time to get silly and use as many of these devices as you can in one sentence. The only rule is that you have to use at least two.

So don't be stingy. Be silly and sprinkle your sentences with as many as you can.

alliteration   simile

hyperbole   metaphor

onomatopoeia   idiom

personification   interjection

_____

_____

_____

_____

_____

_____

_____

Hint: Use a comma instead of an exclamation point after your interjections.

PUTTING IT ALL TOGETHER

Congratulations! Now it's time to show off your new language skills. After all, now that you know what an onomatopoeia is, it would be silly not to use a few.

Follow the prompts and use as many of your new figurative language tools as you can.

DESCRIBE A HOLIDAY DINNER WITH YOUR FAMILY.

TWO GIRAFFES HAVE ESCAPED FROM THE ZOO. DESCRIBE THEIR ADVENTURE.

DESCRIBE THE BEST GIFT THAT YOU'VE EVER GOTTEN.

EXTRA, EXTRA

USE THE NEXT PAGES TO CREATE YOUR OWN STORIES.

JENNIFER WOOLF holds a Master's Degree in writing from USC and has worked as a writer, script reader and story editor. Her true passion is sharing her love of writing and language. As a writing tutor, Jennifer found herself creating her own worksheets for her students, and with lots of feedback from her young students, Jennifer kept tinkering and finally put it all together in one outrageously fun workbook.

Jennifer runs two writing websites at www.figurativewriting.com and www.ccwi.net. She lives in Encino, California with her husband, children, and beagle.